FURTHER POETIC GEMS

FURTHER POETIC GEMS

William McGonagall

Poet and Tragedian

Died in Edinburgh 29th September, 1902

DUCKWORTH

First published in this edition 1980

Gerald Duckworth & Co Ltd
The Old Piano Factory
43 Gloucester Crescent, London NW1

Copyright © 1980 in this edition by
Gerald Duckworth & Co Ltd
All rights reserved

ISBN 0 7156 1510 6

Typeset by Elanders Computer Assisted
Typesetting Systems, Inverness
and printed and bound in Great Britain by
Redwood Burn Limited
Trowbridge and Esher

CONTENTS

	PAGE
To Mr James Scrymgeour, Dundee	7
The Battle of Bannockburn	9
Edinburgh	13
Glasgow	14
Oban	16
The Battle of Flodden Field	18
Greenland's Icy Mountains	22
Tribute to Henry M. Stanley	25
Jottings of New York	26
Beautiful Monikie	28
Death of the Old Mendicant	30
Loch Katrine	32
Forget-Me-Not	33
The Royal Review	35
The Nithsdale Widow and her Son	37
Jack o' the Cudgel	40
The Battle of Culloden	46
The Battle of Sheriffmuir	50
Execution of James Graham, Marquis of Montrose	54
Baldovan	57
Loch Leven	58
The Castle of Mains	59
Montrose	60
Broughty Ferry	61
Robert Burns	62
Adventures of Robert the Bruce	63
A Tale of the Sea	65
Jottings of London	69
Annie Marshall the Foundling	71
Bill Bowls the Sailor	73
Young Munro the Sailor	76
A Tribute to Mr Murphy and the Blue Ribbon Army	79

TO MR JAMES SCRYMGEOUR, DUNDEE

Success to James Scrymgeour,
   He's a very good man,
And to gainsay it,
   There's few people can;

Because he makes the hearts
   Of the poor o'erjoyed
By trying to find work for them
   When they're unemployed.

And to their complaints
   He has always an attentive ear,
And ever ready to help them
   When unto him they draw near.

And no matter what your occupation is,
   Or what is your creed,
He will try to help you
   In the time of need!

Because he has the fear
   Of God within his heart,
And the man that fears God
Always takes the poor's part.

And blessed is the man
   That is kind to the poor!
For his reward in heaven,
   'Tis said in the Scripture, is sure.

And I hope heaven will be
   Mr James Scrymgeour's reward!
For his struggles on behalf of the poor
   Are really vexatious and hard.

For he is to be seen daily
    Walking along our streets,
With a Christian-looking countenance,
    And a kind word to all he meets.

Besides, he is void of all pride,
    And wouldn't feel ashamed
To be seen with a beggar
    Or a tinker walking by his side.

Fellow-citizens of Dundee,
    Isn't it really very nice
To think of James Scrymgeour trying
    To rescue fallen creatures from the paths of vice?

And in the winter he tries to provide
    Hot dinners for the poor children of Dundee,
Who are starving with hunger no doubt,
    And in the most abject poverty.

He is a little deaf, no doubt,
    But not deaf to the cries of hungry men;
No! he always tries to do his best
    To procure bread for them.

And at the Sabbath-morning free-breakfasts
    He is often seen there,
Administering to the wants of the hungry,
    And joining in prayer.

He is a man of noble principles,
    As far as I can think,
And the nobles principle he has got
    Is, he abhors the demon drink.

And, in my opinion, he is right
    As far as I can see,
And I hereby proclaim that such a man
    Is an honour to Dundee:

Because he is always working
    For the poor people's good,
Kind soul, trying hard
    To procure for them clothing and food.

Success to him and his family,
    And may God them defend:
Why? fellow-citizens of Dundee,
    Because he is the poor man's friend.

THE BATTLE OF BANNOCKBURN

Sir Robert the Bruce at Bannockburn
Beat the English in every wheel and turn,
And made them fly in great dismay
From off the field without delay.

The English were a hundred thousand strong,
And King Edward passed through the Lowlands all along,
Determined to conquer Scotland, it was his desire,
And then to restore it to his own empire.

King Edward brought numerous waggons in his train,
Expecting that most of the Scottish army would be slain,
Hoping to make the rest prisoners, and carry them away
In waggon-loads to London without delay.

The Scottish army did not amount to more than thirty
    thousand strong!
But Bruce had confidence he'd conquer his foes ere long;
So, to protect his little army, he thought it was right
To have deep-dug pits made in the night;

And caused them to be overlaid with turf and brushwood
Expecting the plan would prove effectual where his little
    army stood,
Waiting patiently for the break of day,
All willing to join in the deadly fray.

Bruce stationed himself at the head of the reserve,
Determined to conquer, but never to swerve,
And by his side were brave Kirkpatrick and true De Longueville,
Both trusty warriors, firm and bold, who would never him beguile.

By daybreak the whole of the English army came in view,
Consisting of archers and horsemen, bold and true;
The main body was led on by King Edward himself,
an avaricious man, and fond of pelf.

The Abbot of Inchaffray celebrated mass,
And all along the Scottish lines barefoot he did pass,
With the crucifix in his hand, a most beautiful sight to see,
Exhorting them to trust in God, and He would set them free.

Then the Scottish army knelt down on the field,
And King Edward he thought they were going to yield,
And he felt o'erjoyed, and cried to Earl Percy,
"See! See! the Scots are crying for mercy."

But Percy said, "Your Majesty need not make such a fuse,
They are crying for mercy from God, not from us;
For, depend upon it, they will fight to a man, and find their graves
Rather than yield to become your slaves."

Then King Edward ordered his horsemen to charge,
Thirty thousand in number, it was very large;
They thought to o'erwhelm them ere they could rise from their knees,
But they met a different destiny, which did them displease
For the horsemen fell into the spik'd pits in the way,
And, with broken ranks and confusion, they all fled away.

But few of them escap'd death from the spik'd pits,
For the Scots with their swords hack'd them to bits;
De Valence was overthrown and carried off the field
Then King Edward he thought it was time to yield.

And he uttered a fearful cry
To his gay archers near by,
Ho! archers! draw your arrows to the head,
And make sure to kill them dead;
Forward, without dread, and make them fly,
Saint George for England, be our cry!

Then the arrows from their bows swiftly did go,
And fell amongst them as thick as the flakes of snow;
Then Bruce he drew his trusty blade,
And in heroic language said,
Forward! my heroes, bold and true!
And break the archers' ranks through and through!
And charge them boldly with your swords in hand,
And chase these vultures from off our land,
And make King Edward mourn
The day he came to Bannockburn.

See proud Edward on his milk-white steed,
One of England's finest breed,
Coming here in grand array,
With horsemen bold and archers gay,
Thinking he will us dismay,
And sweep everything before him in his way;
But I swear by yon blessed sun
I'll make him and his army run
From off the field of Bannockburn.

By St Andrew and our God most high,
We'll conquer these epicures or die!

And make them fly like chaff before the wind
Until they can no refuge find!
And beat them off the field without delay,
Like lions bold and heroes gay.
Upon them! – charge! – follow me,
For Scotland's rights and liberty!

Then the Scots charged them with sword in hand,
And made them fly from off their land;
And King Edward was amazed at the sight,
And he got wounded in the fight;
And he cried, Oh, heaven! England's lost, and I'm undone,
Alas! alas! where shall I run?
Then he turned his horse, and rode on afar,
And never halted till he reached Dunbar.

Then Bruce he shouted, Victory!
We have gained our rights and liberty;
And thanks be to God above
That we have conquered King Edward this day,
A usurper that does not us love.

Then the Scots did shout and sing,
Long live Sir Robert Bruce our King!
That made King Edward mourn
The day he came to Bannockburn!

EDINBURGH

Beautiful city of Edinburgh!
Where the tourist can drown his sorrow
By viewing your monuments and statues fine
During the lovely summer-time.
I'm sure it will his spirits cheer
As Sir Walter Scott's monument he draws near,
That stands in East princes Street
Amongst flowery gardens, fine and neat.
And Edinburgh castle is magnificent to be seen
With its beautiful walks and trees so green,
Which seems like a fairy dell;
And near by its rocky basement is St Margaret's well,
Where the tourist can drink at when he feels dry,
And view the castle from beneath so very high,
Which seems almost towering to the sky.
Then as for Nelson's monument that stands on the Calton hill,
As the tourist gazes thereon, with wonder his heart does fill
As he thinks on Admiral Nelson who did the Frenchmen kill.
Then, as for Salisbury crags, they are most beautiful to be seen,
Especially in the month of June, when the grass is green;
There numerous mole-hills can be seen,
And the busy little creatures howking away,
Searching for worms amongst the clay;
And as the tourist's eye does wander to and fro
From the south side of Salisbury crags below,
His bosom with admiration feels all aglow
As he views the beautiful scenery in the valley below;
And if, with an observant eye, the little loch beneath he scans,
He can see the wild ducks swimming about and beautiful
    white swans.

Then, as for Arthur's seat, I'm sure it is a treat
Most worthy to be seen, with its rugged rocks and pastures green,
And the sheep browsing on its sides
To and fro, with slow-paced strides,
And the little lambkins at play
During the livelong summer-day.
Beautiful city of Edinburgh! the truth to express,
Your beauties are matchless I must confess,
And which no one dare gainsay,
But that you are the grandest city in Scotland at the present day!

GLASGOW

Beautiful city of Glasgow, with your streets so neat and clean,
Your stately mansions, and beautiful Green!
Likewise your beautiful bridges across the river Clyde,
And on your bonnie banks I would like to reside.

Chorus –
Then away to the West – to the beautiful West!
To the fair city of Glasgow that I like the best,
Where the river Clyde rolls on to the sea,
And the lark and the blackbird whistle with glee.

'Tis beautiful to see the ships passing to and fro,
Laden with goods for the high and the low!
So let the beautiful city of Glasgow flourish,
And may the inhabitants always find food their bodies to nourish.

Chorus

The statue of the Prince of Orange is very grand,
Looking terror to the foe, with a truncheon in his hand,
And well mounted on a noble steed, which stands in the Trongate,
And holding up its foreleg, I'm sure it looks first-rate.

Chorus.

Then there's the Duke of Wellington's statue in Royal Exchange Square —
It is a beautiful statue I without fear declare,
Besides inspiring and most magnificent to view,
Because he made the French fly at the battle of Waterloo.

Chorus.

And as for the statue of Sir Walter Scott that stands in George Square,
It is a handsome statue – few can with it compare,
And most elegant to be seen,
And close beside it stands the statue of Her Majesty the Queen.

Chorus.

Then there's the statue of Robert Burns in George Square,
And the treatment he received when living was very unfair;
Now, when he's dead, Scotland's sons for him do mourn,
But, alas! unto them he can never return.

Chorus.

Then as for Kelvin Grove, it is most lovely to be seen
With its beautiful flowers and trees so green,
And a magnificent water-fountain spouting up very high,
Where the people can quench their thirst when they feel dry.

Chorus.

Beautiful city of Glasgow, I now conclude my muse,
And to write in praise of thee my pen does not refuse;
And, without fear of contradiction, I will venture to say
You are the second grandest city in Scotland at the present day!

Chorus.

OBAN

Oh! beautiful Oban with your lovely bay,
Your surroundings are magnificent on a fine summer-day!
There the lover of the picturesque can behold,
As the sun goes down, the scenery glittering like gold.

And on a calm evening, behind the village let him climb the hill,
And as he watches the sun go down, with delight his heart
   will fill
As he beholds the sun casting a golden track across the sea,
Clothing the dark mountains of Mull with crimson brilliancy.

And on a sunny morning 'tis delightful to saunter up the
   Dunstaffnage road,
Where the green trees spread out their branches so broad;
And as you pass the Lovers' Loan your spirits feel gay
As you see the leaflet float lightly on the sunny pathway.

And when you reach the little gate on the right hand,
Then turn and feast your eyes on the scene most grand,
And there you will see the top of Balloch-an-Righ to your right,
Until at last you will exclaim, Oh! what a beautiful sight!

And your mind with wonder it must fill
As you follow the road a couple of iles further, till
You can see Bennefure Loch on the left hand,
And the Castle of Dunstaffnage most ancient and grand.

Then go and see the waters of Loch Etive leaping and
  thundering
And flashing o'er the reef, splashing and dundering,
Just as they did when Ossian and Fingal watched them from
  the shore,
And, no doubt, they have felt delighted by the rapids'
  thundering roar.

Then there's Ganevan with its sparkling bay,
And its crescent of silver sand glittering in the sun's bright
  array,
And Dunolly's quiet shores where sea crabs abide,
And its beautiful little pools left behind by the tide.

Then take a sail across to Kerrera some day,
And see Gylen Castle with its wild-strewn shore and bay,
With its gigantic walls and towers of rocks
Shivered into ghastly shapes by the big waves' thundering
  shocks.

Then wander up Glen Crootyen, past the old village churchyard,
And as you pass, for the dead have some regard;
For it is the road we've all to go,
Sooner or later, both the high and the low!

And as you return by the side of the merry little stream,
That comes trotting down the glen most charming to be seen,
Sometimes wimpling along between heather banks,
And slipping coyly away to hide itself in its merry pranks.

Then on some pleasant evening walk up the Glen Shellach road,
Where numberless sheep the green hillside often have trod,
And there's a little farmhouse nestling amongst the trees,
And its hazel woods climbing up the brae, shaking in the
  breeze.

And Loch Avoulyen lies like a silver sea with its forests
    green,
With its fields of rushes and headlands most enchanting to
    be seen,
And on the water, like a barge anchored by some dreamland shore,
There wild fowls sit, mirrored, by the score.

And this is beautiful Oban, where the tourist seldom stays
    above a night,
A place that fills the lover of the picturesque with delight;
And let all the people that to Oban go
View it in its native loveliness, and it will drive away all
    woe.

Oh! beautiful Oban, with your silvery bay,
'Tis amongst your Highland scenery I'd like to stray
During the livelong summer-day,
And feast my eyes on your beautiful scenery, enchanting and
    gay.

THE BATTLE OF FLODDEN FIELD

'Twas on the 9th of September, a very beautiful day,
That a mumerous English army came in grand array,
And pitched their tents on Flodden field so green
In the year of our Lord fifteen hundred and thirteen.

And on the ridge of Braxton hill the Scottish army lay,
All beautifully arrayed, and eager for the fray,
And near by stood their noble king on that eventful day,
With a sad and heavy heart, but in it no dismay.

And around him were his nobles, both in church and state,
And they felt a little dispirited regarding the king's fate;
For the independence of bonnie Scotland was at stake,
And if they lost the battle, many a heart would break.

And as King James viewed the enemy he really wondered,
Because he saw by them he was greatly outnumbered,
And he knew that the struggle would be desperate to the last,
And for Scotland's weal or woe the die was cast.

The silence of the gathered armies was very still
Until some horsemen began to gallop about the brow of the
    hill,
Then from rank to rank the signal for attack quickly flew,
And each man in haste to his comrade closely drew.

Then the Scottish artillery opened with a fearful cannonade;
But the English army seemed to be not the least afraid,
And they quickly answered them by their cannon on the plain;
While innocent blood did flow, just like a flood of rain.

But the artillery practice very soon did cease,
Then foe met foe foot to foot, and the havoc did increase,
And, with a wild slogan cry, the Highlanders bounded down
    the hill,
And many of the English vanguard, with their claymores,
    they did kill.

Then, taken by surprise and the suddenness of the attack,
The vanguard of the English army instantly fell back,
But rallied again immediately — to be beaten back once more,
Whilst beneath the Highlanders' claymores they fell by the
    score.

But a large body of horsemen came to the rescue,
And the wing of the Scottish army they soon did subdue;
Then swords and spears clashed on every side around,
While the still air was filled with a death-wailing sound.

Then King James thought he'd strike an effective blow —
So he ordered his bodyguard to the plain below,
And all the nobles that were in his train,
To engage the foe hand to hand on that bloody plain.

And to them the din of battle was only a shout of glory;
But for their noble king they felt a little sorry,
Because they knew he was sacrificing a strong position,
Which was to his army a very great acquisition.

But King James was resolved to have his own will,
And he wouldn't allow the English to come up the hill,
Because he thought he wasn't matching himself equally
   against the foe;
So the nobles agreed to follow their leader for weal or woe.

'Twas then they plunged down into the thick of the fight,
And the king fought like a lion with all his might;
And in his cause he saw his nobles falling on every side around,
While he himself had received a very severe wound.

And the English archers were pouring in their shafts like hail
And swords and spears were shivered against coats of mail,
And the king was manfully engaged contesting every inch of
   ground,
While the cries of the dying ascended up to heaven with a
   pitiful sound.

And still around the king the battle fiercely raged,
While his devoted followers were hotly engaged,
And the dead and the dying were piled high all around,
And alas! the brave king had received the second wound.

The Scottish army was composed of men from various
    northern isles,
Who had travelled, no doubt, hundreds of miles;
And with hunger and fatigue many were like to faint,
But the brave heroes uttered no complaint.

And heroically they fought that day on behalf of their king,
Whilst around him they formed a solid ring;
And the king was the hero of the fight,
Cutting, hacking, and slashing left and right.

But alas! they were not proof against the weapons of the foe,
Which filled their hearts with despair and woe;
And, not able to maintain their close form, they were beaten
    back,
And Lennox and Argyle, their leaders, were slain, alack!

And the field became so slippery with blood they could
    scarcely stand,
But in their stocking-feet they fought hand to hand,
And on both sides men fell like wheat before the mower,
While the cheers from both armies made a hideous roar.

Then King James he waved his sword on high,
And cried, "Scotchmen, forward! and make the Saxons fly;
And remember Scotland's independence is at stake,
So charge them boldly for Scotland's sake."

So grooms, lords, and knights fought all alike,
And hard blows for bonnie Scotland they did strike,
And swords and spears loudly did clatter,
And innocent blood did flow like water.

But alas! the king and his nobles fought in vain,
And by an English billman the king was slain;
Then a mighty cheer from the English told Scotland's power had fled,
And King James the Fourth of Scotland, alas! was dead!

GREENLAND'S ICY MOUNTAINS

Greenland's icy mountains are fascinating and grand,
And wondrously created by the Almighty's command;
And the works of the Almighty there's few can understand:
Who knows but it might be a part of Fairyland?

Because there are churches of ice, and houses glittering like glass,
And for scenic grandeur there's nothing can it surpass,
Besides there's monuments and spires, also ruins,
Which serve for a safe retreat from the wild bruins.

And there's icy crags and precipices, also beautiful waterfalls,
And as the stranger gazes thereon, his heart it appals
With a mixture of wonder, fear, and delight,
Till at last he exclaims, Oh! what a wonderful sight!

The icy mountains they're higher than a brig's topmast,
And the stranger in amazement stands aghast
As he beholds the water flowing off the melted ice
Adown the mountain sides, that he cries out, Oh! how nice!

Such sights as these are truly magnificent to be seen,
Only that the mountain tops are white instead of green,
And rents and caverns in them, the same as on a rugged
   mountain side,
And suitable places, in my opinion, for mermaids to reside.

Sometimes these icy mountains suddenly topple o'er
With a wild and rumbling hollow-startling roar;
And new peaks and cliffs rise up out of the sea,
While great cataracts of uplifted brine pour down furiously.

And those that can witness such an awful sight
Can only gaze thereon in solemn silence and delight,
And the most Godfearless man that hath this region trod
Would be forced to recognise the power and majesty of God.

Oh! how awful and grand it must be on a sunshiny day
To see one of these icy mountains in pieces give way!
While, crack after crack, it falls with a mighty crash
Flat upon the sea with a fearful splash.

And in the breaking up of these mountains they roar like
   thunder,
Which causes the stranger no doubt to wonder;
Also the Esquimaux of Greenland betimes will stand
And gaze on the wondrous work of the Almighty so grand.

When these icy mountains are falling, the report is like big
   guns,
And the glittering brilliancy of them causes mock-suns,
And around them there's connected a beautiful ring of light,
And as the stranger looks thereon, it fills his heart with delight.

Oh! think on the danger of seafaring men
If any of these mighty mountains were falling on them;
Alas! they would be killed ere the hand of man could them save
And, poor creatures, very likely find a watery grave!

'Tis most beautiful to see and hear the whales whistling and
    blowing,
And the sailors in their small boats quickly after them
    rowing,
While the whales keep lashing the water all their might
With their mighty tails, left and right.

In winter there's no sunlight there night or day,
Which, no doubt, will cause the time to pass tediously away,
And cause the Esquimaux to long for the light of day,
So as they will get basking themselves in the sun's bright array.

In summer there is perpetual sunlight,
Which fill the Esquimaux' hearts with delight;
And is seen every day and night in the blue sky,
Which makes the scenery appear most beautiful to the eye.

During summer and winter there the land is covered with snow,
Which sometimes must fill the Esquimaux' hearts with woe
As they traverse fields of ice, ten or fifteen feet thick,
And with cold, no doubt, their hearts will be touched to the
    quick.

And let those that read or hear this feel thankful to God
That the icy fields of Greenland they have never trod;
Especially while seated around the fireside on a cold winter
    night,
Let them think of the cold and hardships Greenland sailors
    have to fight.

TRIBUTE TO HENRY M. STANLEY, THE GREAT AFRICAN EXPLORER

Welcome, thrice welcome, to the City of Dundee
The great African explorer, Henry M Stanley,
Who went out to Africa its wild regions to explore,
And travelled o'er wild and lonely deserts, fatigued and footsore.

And what he and his little band suffered will never be forgot
Especially one in particular, Major Edmund Barttelot,
Alas! the brave heroic officer by a savage was shot,
The commandant of the rear column — O hard has been his lot!

O think of the noble Stanley and his gallant little band,
While travelling through gloomy forests and devastated land
And suffering from all kinds of hardships under a burning sun!
But the brave hero has been successful, and the victory's won!

While in Africa he saw many wonderful sights,
And was engaged, no doubt, in many savage fights,
But the wise Creator was with him all along,
And now he's home again to us, I hope quite strong.

And during his travels in Africa he made strange discoveries,
He discovered a dwarfish race of people called pigmies,
Who are said to be the original natives of Africa,
And when Stanley discovered them he was struck with awe.

One event in particular is most worthy to relate,
How God preserved him from a very cruel fate:
He and his officers were attacked, while sailing in their boat,
By the savages of Bumbireh, all eager to cut his throat.

They seized him by the hair, and tugged it without fear,
While one of his men received a poke in the ribs with a spear;
But Stanley, having presence of mind, instantly contrives
To cry to his men, Shove off the boat, and save your lives!

Then savages swarmed into three canoes very close by,
And every bow was drawn, while they savagely did cry;
But the heroic Stanley quickly shot two of them dead,
Then the savages were baffled, and immediately fled.

This incident is startling, but nevertheless true,
And in the midst of all dangers, the Lord brought him through,
Then, welcome him, thrice welcome him, right cheerfully,
Shouting, Long live the great African explorer, Henry M
   Stanley!

Therefore throw open the gates of the City of Dundee,
And receive him with loud cheers, three times three,
And sound your trumpets and beat your drums,
And play up, See the Conquering Hero Comes!

JOTTINGS OF NEW YORK

Oh mighty City of New York! you are wonderful to behold,
Your buildings are magnificent, the truth be it told,
They were the only thing that seemed to arrest my eye,
Because many of them are thirteen storeys high.

And as for Central Park, it is lovely to be seen,
Especially in the summer season when its shrubberies and
   trees are green;
And the Burns' statue is there to be seen,
Surrounded by trees, on the beautiful sward so green;
Also, Shakespeare and Sir Walter Scott,
Which by Englishmen and Scotchmen will ne'er be forgot.

There the people on the Sabbath-day in thousands resort,
All loud in conversation and searching for sport,
Some of them viewing the menagerie of wild beasts there,
And also beautiful black swans, I do declare.

And there's beautiful boats to be seen there,
And the joyous shouts of the children do rend the air,
While the boats sail along with them o'er Lohengrin Lake,
And the fare is five cents for children and adults ten is all
    they take.

And there's also summer-house shades and merry-go-rounds,
And with the merry laughter of the children the Park resounds
During the livelong Sabbath-day,
Enjoying the merry-go-round play.

Then there's the elevated railroads, about five storeys high,
Which the inhabitants can see and hear night and day
    passing by,
Oh! such a mass of people daily do throng,
No less than five hundred thousand daily pass along,
And all along the City you can get for five cents,
And, believe me, among the passengers there are few
    discontent.

And the tops of the houses are all flat,
And in the warm weather the people gather to chat,
Besides on the house-tops they dry their clothes,
And also many people all night on the house-tops repose.

And numerous ships and steamboats are there to be seen
Sailing along the East River Water so green;
'Tis certainly a most beautiful sight
To see them sailing o'er the smooth water day and night.

And Brooklyn Bridge is a very great height,
And fills the stranger's heart with wonder at first sight,
But with all its loftiness, I venture to say,
For beauty it cannot surpass the new Railway Bridge of the
    Silvery Tay.

And there's also ten thousand rumsellers there,
Oh! wonderful to think, I do declare!
To accommodate the people of that city therein,
And to encourage them to commit all sorts of sin.

And on the Sabbath-day, ye will see many a man
Going for beer with a tin can,
And seems proud to be seen carrying home the beer
To treat his neighbours and family dear.

Then at night numbers of the people dance and sing,
Making the walls of their houses to ring
With their songs and dancing on Sabbath night,
Which I witnessed with disgust, and fled from the sight.

And with regard to New York and the sights I did see,
One street in Dundee is more worth to me,
And, believe me, the morning I sailed from New York
For Bonnie Dundee, my heart it felt as light as a cork.

BEAUTIFUL MONIKIE

Beautiful Monikie! with your trees and shrubberies green,
And your beautiful walks, most charming to be seen:
'Tis a beautiful place for pleasure-seekers to resort,
Because there they can have innocent sport,
By taking a leisure walk all round about,
And see the anglers fishing in the pond for trout.

Besides, there's lovely white swans swimming on the pond,
And Panmure Monument can be seen a little distance beyond!
And the scenery all round is enchanting I declare,
While sweet-scented fragrance fills the air.

Then away, pleasure-seekers of bonnie Dundee,
And have a day's outing around Monikie,
And inhale the pure air, on a fine summer day,
Which will help to drive dull care away;
As ye gaze on the beautiful scenery there,
Your spirits will feel o'erjoyed and free from care.

Then near to the pond there's a beautiful green sward,
Where excursionists can dance until fatigue does them retard:
And if they feel thirsty, the Monikie water's near by,
Where they can quench their thirst if very dry.

Then, after that, they can have a walk at their ease,
Amongst the green shrubbery and tall pine trees;
And the centre of the pond they can see
Three beautiful little islets dressed in green livery.

Monikie is as bonnie a place as ye could wish to see,
And about eleven or twelve miles from bonnie Dundee;
It's the only place I know of to enjoy a holiday,
Because there's a hall of shelter there to keep the rain away.

Then there's a large park, a very suitable place,
For the old and the young, if they wish to try a race;
It's there they can enjoy themselves during the live-long
    summer day,
Near to the little purling burn, meandering on its way,
And emptying itself into the pond of Monikie,
Which supplies the people with water belonging Dundee.

DEATH OF THE OLD MENDICANT

There was a rich old gentleman
Lived on a lonely moor in Switzerland,
And he was very hard to the wandering poor,
'Tis said he never lodged nor served them at his door.

'Twas on a stormy night, and Boreas blew a bitter blast,
And the snowflakes they fell thick and fast,
When a poor old mendicant, tired and footsore,
Who had travelled that day fifteen miles and more,
Knocked loudly at the rich man's door.

The rich man was in his parlour counting his gold,
And he ran to the door to see who was so bold,
And there he saw the mendicant shivering with the cold

Then the mendicant unto him said,
My dear sir, be not afraid,
Pray give me lodgings for the night,
And heaven will your love requite;
Have pity on me, for I am tired and footsore,
I have travelled fifteen miles to-day and more.

Begone! you vagabond, from my door!
I never give lodgings to the poor;
So be off, take to your heels and run,
Or else I'll shoot you with my gun!
Now do not think I'm making fun;
Do you hear, old beggar, what I say?
Now be quick! and go away.

Have mercy, sir, I cannot go,
For I shall perish in the snow;
Oh! for heaven's sake, be not so hard,
And God will your love reward.

My limbs are tired, I cannot go away,
Oh! be so kind as let me stay.
'Twas vain! the rich man said, I shan't,
And shut his door on the mendicant,
And said, That is the way I'll serve the poor
While I live on this lonely moor.

Then the old mendicant did go away,
And, murmuring to himself, did say,
Oh, woe's me that ever I was born!
Oh, God, protect me from the storm
My feeble limbs refuse to go,
And my poor heart does break with woe.

Then he lay down and died among the snow.
He was found by the rich man's shepherd next day,
While he was searching for sheep that had gone astray
And he was struck with fear and woe
To see the body lying dead among the snow.

So the shepherd ran home and told his master
About the very sad disaster;
That he had found a dead body in the snow,
But whose it was he did not know.

Then the rich man ordered the body to be brought to his house
And to be instantly dressed by his loving spouse,
For his conscience smote him with fear and woe,
When he heard of the old mendicant being found dead in
   the snow.

So the poor old mendicant was buried without delay
In a very respectable way;
And from that very day the rich man was kind to the poor
And never turned any one away from his door.

LOCH KATRINE

Beautiful Loch Katrine in all thy majesty so grand,
Oh! how charming and fascinating is thy silver strand!
Thou certainly art most lovely, and worthy to be seen,
Especially thy beautiful bay and shrubberies green.

    Then away to Loch Katrine in the summer time,
    And feast on its scenery most lovely and sublime;
    There's no other scene can surpass in fair Scotland,
    It's surrounded by mountains and trees most grand.

And as I gaze upon it, let me pause and think,
How many people in Glasgow of its water drink,
That's conveyed to them in pipes from its placid lake,
And are glad to get its water their thirst to slake.

    Then away to Loch Katrine in the summer time,
    And feast on its scenery most lovely and sublime;
    There's no other scene can surpass in fair Scotland,
    It's surrounded by mountains and trees most grand.

The mountains on either side of it are beautiful to be seen,
Likewise the steamers sailing on it with their clouds of steam:
And their shadows on its crystal waters as they pass along,
Is enough to make the tourist burst into song.

    Then away to Loch Katrine in the summer time,
    And feast on its scenery most lovely and sublime;
    There's no other scene can surpass in fair Scotland,
    It's surrounded by mountains and trees most grand.

'Tis beautiful to see its tiny wimpling rills,
And the placid Loch in the hollow of a circle of hills,
Glittering like silver in the sun's bright array,
Also many a promontory, little creek, and bay.

Then away to Loch Katrine in the summer time,
And feast on its scenery most lovely and sublime;
There's no other scene can surpass in fair Scotland,
It's surrounded by mountains and trees most grand.

Then to the east there's the finely wooded Ellen's Isle,
There the tourist can the tedious hours beguile,
As he gazes on its white gravelled beautiful bay,
It will help to drive dull care away.

Then away to Loch Katrine in the summer time,
And feast on its scenery most lovely and sublime;
There's no other scene can surpass in fair Scotland,
It's surrounded by mountains and trees most grand.

The mountains Ben-An and Ben-Venue are really very grand,
Likewise the famous and clear silver strand;
Where the bold Rob Roy spent many a happy day,
With his faithful wife, near by its silvery bay.

Then away to Loch Katrine in the summer time,
And feast on its scenery most lovely and sublime;
There's no other scene can surpass in fair Scotland,
It's surrounded by mountains and trees most grand.

FORGET-ME-NOT

A gallant knight and his betroth'd bride,
Were walking one day by a river side,
They talk'd of love, and they talk'd of war,
And how very foolish lovers are.

At length the bride to the knight did say,
There have been many young ladies led astray
By believing in all their lovers said,
And you are false to me I am afraid.

No, Ellen, I was never false to thee,
I never gave thee cause to doubt me;
I have always lov'd thee and do still,
And no other woman your place shall fill.

Dear Edwin, it may be true, but I am in doubt,
But there's some beautiful flowers here about,
Growing on the other side of the river,
But how to get one, I cannot discover.

Dear Ellen, they seem beautiful indeed,
But of them, dear, take no heed;
Because they are on the other side,
Besides, the river is deep and wide.

Dear Edwin, as I doubt your love to be untrue,
I ask one favour now from you:
Go! fetch me a flower from across the river,
Which will prove you love me more than ever.

Dear Ellen! I will try and fetch you a flower
If it lies within my power   *   *   *
To prove that I am true to you,
And what more can your Edwin do?

So he leap'd into the river wide,
And swam across to the other side,
To fetch a flower for his young bride,
Who watched him eagerly on the other side.

So he pluck'd a flower right merrily,
Which seemed to fill his heart with glee,
That it would please his lovely bride;
But, alas! he never got to the other side.

For when he tried to swim across,
All power of his body he did loss,
But before he sank in the river wide,
He flung the flowers to his lovely bride.

And he cried, Oh, Heaven! hard is my lot,
My dearest Ellen! Forget me not:
For I was ever true to you,
My dearest Ellen! I bid thee adieu!

Then she wrung her hands in wild despair,
Until her cries did rend the air;
And she cried, Edwin, dear, hard is our lot,
But I'll name this flower Forget-me-not.

And I'll remember thee while I live,
And to no other man my hand I'll give,
And I will place my affection on this little flower,
And it will solace me in a lonely hour

THE ROYAL REVIEW, AUGUST 25, 1881

All hail to the Empress of India, Great Britain's Queen—
Long may she live in health, happy and seren—
That came from London, far away,
To review the Scottish Volunteers in grand array:
Most magnificent to be seen,
Near by Salisbury Crags and its pastures green,
Which will long be remembered by our gracious Queen—

And by the Volunteers, that came from far away,
Because it rain'd most of the day.
And with the rain their clothes were wet all through,
On the 25th day of August, at the Royal Review.
And to the Volunteers it was no lark,
Because they were ankle deep in mud in the Queen's Park,
Which proved to the Queen they were loyal and true,
To endure such hardships at the Royal Review.

Oh! it was a most beautiful scene
To see the Forfarshire Artillery marching past the Queen;
Her Majesty with their steady marching felt content,
Especially when their arms to her they did present.

And the Inverness Highland Volunteers seemed verygran',
And marched by steady to a man
Amongst the mud without dismay,
And the rain pouring down on them all the way.
And the bands they did play, God Save the Queen,
Near by Holyrood Palace and the Queen's Park so green.

Success to our noble Scottish Volunteers!
I hope they will be spared for many long years,
And to Her Majesty always prove loyal and true.
As they have done for the second time at the Royal Review.

To take them in general, they behaved very well,
The more that the rain fell on them pell-mell.
They marched by Her Majesty in very grand array,
Which will be remembered for many a long day,
Bidding defiance to wind and rain,
Which adds the more fame to their name.

And I hope none of them will have cause to rue
The day that they went to the Royal Review.
And I'm sure Her Majesty ought to feel proud,
And in their praise she cannot speak too loud,
Because the more that it did rain they did not mourn,
Which caused Her Majesty's heart with joy to burn,
Because she knew they were loyal and true
For enduring such hardships at the Royal Review.

THE NITHSDALE WIDOW AND HER SON

'Twas in the year of 1746, on a fine summer afternoon,
When trees and flowers were in full bloom,
That widow Riddel sat knitting stockings on a little rustic seat,
Which her only son had made for her, which was very neat.

The cottage she lived in was in the wilds of Nithsdale,
Where many a poor soul had cause to bewail
The loss of their shealings, that were burned to the ground,
By a party of fierce British dragoons that chanced to come round.

While widow Riddel sat in her garden she heard an unusual sound,
And near by was her son putting some seeds into the ground,
And as she happened to look down into the little strath below,
She espied a party of dragoons coming towards her very slow.

And hearing of the cruelties committed by them, she shook with fear.
And she cried to her son, "Jamie, thae sodgers are coming here!"
While the poor old widow's heart with fear was panting,
And she cried, "Mercy on us, Jamie, what can they be wanting?"

Next minute the dragoons were in front of the cottage door,
When one of them dismounted, and loudly did roar,
"Is there any rebels, old woman, skulking hereabouts?"
"Oh, no, Sir, no! believe my word without any doubts."

"Well, so much the better, my good woman, for you and them;
But, old girl, let's have something to eat, me, and my men":
"Blithely, sir, blithely! ye're welcome to what I hae,"
When she bustled into the cottage without delay.

And she brought out oaten cakes, sweet milk, and cheese,
Which the soldiers devoured greedily at their ease,
And of which they made a hearty meal,
But, for such kind treatment, ungrateful they did feel.

Then one of the soldiers asked her how she got her living:
She replied, "God unto her was always giving;
And wi' the bit garden, alang wi' the bit coo,
And wi' what the laddie can earn we are sincerely thankfu'."

To this pitiful detail of her circumstances the villain made
    no reply,
But drew a pistol from his holster, and cried, "your cow
    must die!"
Then riding up to the poor cow, discharged it through her
    head,
When the innocent animal instantly fell down dead.

Not satisfied with this the merciless ruffian leaped the little
    garden wall,
And with his horse trod down everything, the poor widow's all,
Then having finished this barbarous act of direst cruelty,
The monster rejoined his comrades shouting right merrily:

"There, you old devil, that's what you really deserve,
For you and your rascally rebels ought to starve";
Then the party rode off, laughing at the mischief that was
    done,
Leaving the poor widow to mourn and her only son.

When the widow found herself deprived of her all,
She wrung her hands in despair, and on God did call,
Then rushed into the cottage and flung herself on her bed,
And, with sorrow, in a few days she was dead.

And, during her illness, her poor boy never left her bedside,
There he remained, night and day, his mother's wants to provide,
And make her forget the misfortunes that had befallen them,
All through that villainous and hard-hearted party of men.

On the fourth day her son followed her remains to the grave.
And during the burial service he most manfully did behave,
And when the body was laid in the grave, from tears he could not refrain,
But instantly fled from that desolated place, and never returned again.

Thirteen years after this the famous battle of Minden was fought
By Prince Ferdinand against the French, who brought them to nought;
And there was a large body of British horse, under Lord George Sackville,
And strange! the widow's son was at the battle all the while.

And on the evening after the battle there were assembled in a tavern
A party of British dragoons, loudly boasting and swearing,
When one of them swore he had done more than any of them —
A much more meritorious action — which he defied them to condemn.

"What was that, Tam, what was that, Tam?" shouted his companions at once.
"Tell us, Tam; tell us, Tam, was that while in France?"
"No!" he cried, "it was starving an old witch, while in Nithsdale,
By shooting her cow and riding down her greens, that is the tale."

"And don't you repent it?" exclaimed a young soldier,
present.
"Repent what?" cried the braggart; "No! I feel quite
content."
"Then, villain!" cried the youth, unsheathing his sword,
"That woman was my mother, so not another word!

"So draw, and defend yourself, without more delay,
For I swear you shall not live another day!"
Then the villain sprang to his feet, and a combat ensued,
But in three passes he was entirely subdued.

Young Riddel afterwards rose to be a captain
In the British service, and gained a very good name
For being a daring soldier, wherever he went,
And as for killing the ruffian dragoon he never did repent.

JACK O' THE CUDGEL

PART I

'Twas in the famous town of Windsor, on a fine summer morn,
Where the sign of Windsor Castle did a tavern adorn;
And there sat several soldiers drinking together,
Resolved to make merry in spite of wind or weather.

And old Simon the landlord was at the head of the table,
Cutting slices of beef as quick as he was able;
And one of the soldiers was of rather superior rank,
And on his dress trinkets of gold and silver together did clank.

He was a free companion, but surly and hard,
And a soldier of fortune, and was named Croquard;
And he had all the appearance of his martial calling,
But on this particular morning he was rudely bawling.

So the other soldiers laughed, for their spirits felt gay,
And they applauded his jokes, and let him have his own way,
Because he could command as desperate a gang of men as
    any in the world,
So many a joke and slur at the soldiers he hurled.

And the mirth increased as the day wore on,
And Croquard didn't seem the least woe-begone;
But, as he was trolling out a very merry song,
A wandering minstrel sat down beside him, and thought it
    no wrong.

By my troth, shouted Croquard, Come here, minstrel,
And give us a stave of love, or war, which is my will:
But the minstrel didn't appear to comply with this request,
And he tried to withdraw, as he thought it was best.

Ho! didst thou hear me, varlet? then Croquard did cry;
Oh! gentle sir, replied the minstrel, I cannot with your wish
    comply;
Believe me, I sing best to the ladies at the court,
And, in doing so, find it more profitable sport.

What, varlet! cried Croquard, Dost thou refuse me?
By heaven, proud cur, you shall see
And feel the weight of my hand before thou are much older:
Then he instantly sprang up, and seized the minstrel by the
    shoulder.

Then the youth began to tremble, and seemed terrified to
    death,
And appeared ready to faint for the want of breath;
While Croquard shook him roughly, just like an ugly whelp
And he looked from one to another, imploring help.

At this moment a youth observed what was going on,
And he cried out to Croquard, Inhuman monster, begone!
Leave the minstrel, thou pig-headed giant, or I'll make you
    repent,
For thou must know my name is Jack, and I hail from Kent.

Then Croquard relaxed his hold of the minstrel boy,
Which caused the minstrel's heart to leap with joy;
As Jack placed himself before Croquard the giant,
And stood on his guard with a stout oak cudgel defiant.

Then the fist of the giant descended in a crack,
But Jack dealt Croquard a heavy blow upon the back
With his cudgel, so that the giant's hand fell powerless down
    by his side,
And he cursed and roared with pain, and did Jack deride.

Then the giant tried to draw his sword for to fight,
But Jack danced around him like a young sprite,
And struck him a blow with his cudgel upon the back of the
    head,
And from the effects of the blow he was nearly killed dead.

Then down sank the carcase of the giant to the ground,
While the soldiers about Jack did quickly gather round;
And Jack cried, Ha! lie thou there overgrown brute,
And defiantly he spurned Croquard's body with his foot.

There, lad, cried Vintner Simon, thou hast shown English
    spirit to-day,
By chastising yon overbearing giant in a very proper way;
So come, my lad, and drink a flagon of my very best sack,
For you handled your cudgel well, and no courage did lack

Then no sooner had our hero finished his goblet of sack,
He cried, Go and fetch the minstrel back;
For the giant by this time had fled far away,
Therefore the minstrel's tender heart need not throb with
   dismay.

Then the minstrel was brought back without delay,
Which made Jack's heart feel light and gay;
And the minstrel thanked Jack for saving him on that
   eventful day,
So the soldiers drank to Jack's health, and then went away.

And when King Edward III. heard what Jack had done,
He sent for Jack o' the Cudgel, the noble Saxon,
And he made him his page, and Jack uttered not a word,
But he unwillingly gave up the cudgel for the honour of the
   sword.

PART II

After the battle of Calais, King Edward returns to fair
   England,
And he invited his nobles to a banquet most grand,
That the like hadn't been in England for many a day;
And many of the guests invited had come from far away.

The large hall of Windsor Castle was ablaze with light,
And there sat King Edward and his Queen, a most beautiful
   sight—
To see them seated upon two thrones of burnished gold;
And near the King sat Jack o' the Cudgel, like a warrior bold.

And when the banquet was prepared, King Edward arose,
And said, My honoured guests, I have called you together
   for a special purpose!
To celebrate our heroic troops at the charge of the lance.
By my noble and heroic troops at the charge of the lance.

And now, since the war in France with us is o'er,
And Edward, our son, about to marry the lady he does adore,
The most amiable and lovely Countess of Kent;
Therefore, I hope they will live happy together and never repent.

Then King Edward took the Countess by the hand, and said,
Come, Edward, take your bride by the hand, and don't be afraid;
And do not think, my beloved son, that with you I feel wroth,
Therefore, take the Countess by the hand, and plight your troth

Then the Prince arose and took the fair Countess by the hand,
As King Edward, his father, had given the royal command;
Then he led the Countess Joan to the foot of the throne,
Then King Edward and his Queen welcomed the Countess to their palatial home.

Then the Prince unto his father said, I must not forget whatever betide,
That to Sir Jack o' the Cudgel I do owe my bride;
Because he rescued her from the hands of a fierce brigand,
Therefore 'twould be hard to find a braver knight in fair England.

Then a cheer arose, which made the lofty hall to ring,
As Jack advanced towards the throne, on the motion of the King;
Then Jack fell on one knee before King Edward,
Then said the Monarch, Arise, brave youth, and I will thee reward.

Sir Jack, I give thee land to the value of six hundred marks
In thine own native county of Kent, with beautiful parks,
Also beautiful meadows and lovely flowers and trees,
Where you can reside and enjoy yourself as you please.

And remember, when I need your service you will be at my
   command,
Then Jack o' the Cudgel bowed assent, and kissed King
   Edward's hand;
Then the Countess Joan took a string of rarest pearls from
   her hair,
And placed the pearls around Jack's neck, most costly and
   rare.

Then the tumult became uproarious when Jack received the
   presentation,
And he thanked the Lady Joan for the handsome donation;
Then all the ladies did loudly cheer, and on Jack smilingly
   did fan,
And Sir Walter Manny cried aloud, Sir Jack, you are a
   lucky man.

Then the mirth increased, and louder the applause,
And the Countess Joan asked, after a pause,
Tell me who had gained the love of the Knight o' the Cudgel;
Then Jack replied, My lady, you know her right well.

She is the lovely daughter of noble John of Aire,
Then, replied the Countess, she is a lovely creature, I must
   declare;
And I hope the choice that you have made won't make you
Then Jack kissed the Countess's hand, and took his leave.

And he wended his way to his beautiful estate in Kent,
And many a happy day there he spent;
And he married the lovely daughter of John of Aire,
And they lived happy together, and free from all care.

THE BATTLE OF CULLODEN

Twas in the year of 1746, and in April the 14th day,
That Prince Charles Stuart and his army marched on without
 delay,
And on the 14th of April they encamped on Culloden Moor,
But the army felt hungry, and no food could they procure.

And the calls of hunger could not brook delay,
So they resolved to have food, come what may;
They, poor men, were hungry and in sore distress,
And many of them, as well as officers, slipped off to Inverness

The Prince gave orders to bring provisions to the field,
Because he knew without food his men would soon yield
To the pangs of hunger, besides make them feel discontent,
So some of them began to search the neighbourhood for
 refreshment.

And others, from exhaustion, lay down on the ground,
And soon in the arms of Morpheus they were sleeping sound;
While the Prince and some of his officers began to search for
 food,
And got some bread and whisky, which they thought very
 good.

The Highland army was drawn up in three lines in grand
 array,
All eager for the fray in April the 16th day,
Consisting of the Athole Brigade, who made a grand display
On the field of Culloden on that ever-memorable day.

Likewise the Camerons, Stewarts, and Macintoshes, Maclachians
and Macleans,
And John Roy Stewart's regiment, united into one, these
are their names;
Besides the Macleods, Chisholms, Macdonalds of Clanranald
and Glengarry,
Also the noble chieftain Keppoch, all eager the English to
harry.

The second line of the Highland army formed in column on
the right,
Consisting of the Gordons, under Lord Lewis Gordon, ready
for the fight;
Besides the French Royal Scots, the Irish Piquets or Brigade,
Also Lord Kilmarnock's Foot Guards, and a grand show they
made.

Lord John Drummond's regiment and Glenbucket's were
flanked on the right.
By Fitz-James's Dragoons and Lord Elcho's Horse Guards,
a magnificent sight;
And on the left by the Perth squadron under Lord Strathallan,
A fine body of men, and resolved to fight to a man.

And there was Pitsligo, and the Prince's body guards under
Lord Balmerino,
And the third line was commanded by General Stapleton, a
noble hero;
Besides, Lord Ogilvy was in command of the third line or
reserve,
Consisting of the Duke of Perth's regiment and Lord
Ogilvy's – men of firm nerve.

The Prince took his station on a very small eminence,
Surrounded by a troop of Fitz-James's horse for his defence,
Where he had a complete view of the whole field of battle,
Where he could see the front line and hear the cannons rattle.

Both armies were about the distance of a mile from each other,
All ready to commence the fight, brother against brother,
Each expecting that the other would advance
To break a sword in combat, or shiver a lance.

To encourage his men the Duke of Cumberland rode along the line,
Addressing himself hurriedly to every regiment, which was really sublime;
Telling his men to use their bayonets, and allow the Highlanders to mingle with them,
And look terror to the rebel foe, and have courage, my men.

Then Colonel Belford of the Duke's army opened fire from the front line,
After the Highlanders had been firing for a short time;
The Duke ordered Colonel Belford to continue the cannonade,
To induce the Highlanders to advance, because they seemed afraid.

And with a cannon-ball the Prince's horse was shot above the knee,
So that Charles had to change him for another immediately;
And one of his servants who led the horse was killed on the spot,
Which by Prince Charles Stuart was never forgot.

'Tis said in history, before the battle began
The Macdonalds claimed the right as their due of leading
   the van,
And because they wouldn't be allowed, with anger their
   hearts did burn,
Because Bruce conferred that honour upon the Macdonalds
   at the battle of Bannockburn.

And galled beyond endurance by the fire of the English that
   day,
Which caused the Highlanders to cry aloud to be led forward
   without delay,
Until at last the brave Clan Macintosh rushed forward without
   dismay,
While with grape-shot from a side battery hundreds were
   swept away.

Then the Athole Highlanders and the Camerons rushed in
   sword in hand,
And broke through Barrel's and Monro's regiments, a sight
   most grand;
After breaking through these two regiments they gave up
   the contest,
Until at last they had to retreat after doing their best.

Then, stung to the quick, the brave Keppoch, who was
   abandoned by his clan,
Boldly advanced with his drawn sword in hand, the brave
   man.
But, alas! he was wounded by a musket-shot, which he
   manfully bore,
And in the fight he received another shot, and fell to rise
   no more

Nothing could be more disastrous to the Prince that day,
Owing to the Macdonalds refusing to join in the deadly fray;
Because if they had all shown their wonted courage that day,
The proud Duke of Cumberland's army would have been
 forced to run away.

And, owing to the misconduct of the Macdonalds, the
 Highlanders had to yield,
And General O'Sullivan laid hold of Charles's horse, and led
 him off the field,
As the whole army was now in full retreat,
And with the deepest concern the Prince lamented his sore
 defeat.

Prince Charles Stuart, of fame and renown,
You might have worn Scotland's crown,
If the Macdonalds and Glengarry at Culloden had proved
 true;
But, being too ambitious for honour, that they didn't do,
Which, I am sorry to say, proved most disastrous to you,
Looking to the trials and struggles you passed through.

THE BATTLE OF SHERIFFMUIR

'Twas in the year 1715, and on the 10th of November,
Which the people of Scotland have cause to remember;
On that day the Earl of Mar left Perth bound for Sheriffmuir,
At the same time leaving behind a garrison under Colonel
 Balfour.

Besides leaving a force of about three thousand men
    quartered in different parts of Fife,
To protect the people's property, and quell party strife,
The army along with him amounted to three thousand foot
    and twelve hundred cavalry,
All in the best of order, a most pleasant sight to see.

The two armies bivouacked near Sheriffmuir during the night,
And around their camp-fires they talked concerning the
    coming fight.
The Duke of Argyle's English army numbered eight thousand
    strong,
Besides four hundred horse, posted in the rear all along.

And the centre of the first line was composed of ten battalions
    of foot,
Consisting of about four thousand, under the command of
    Clanranald and Glengarry to boot;
And at the head of these battalions Sir John Maclean and
    Brigadier Ogilvie,
And the two brothers of Sir Donald Macdonald of Sleat, all
    in high glee.

The Marquis of Huntly's squadron of horse was also there;
Likewise the Stirling squadron, carrying the Chevalier's
    standard, I do declare;
And the Perthshire squadron formed the left wing,
And with their boisterous shouts they made the welkin ring.

The centre of the second line consisted of eight battalions of
    infantry,
And three of the Earl of Seaforth's foot, famous for their
    bravery;
There were also two battalions of the Marquis of Huntly,
Besides the Earl of Panmure's battalion, all men of high degree.

And those of the Marquis of Tullibardine, commanded by the
  Viscount of Strathallan,
And of Logie Almond, and likewise Robertson of Strowan;
Besides two squadrons of horse under the Earl Marischal,
And the Angus squadron was on the left: these include
  them all.

During this formation, the Duke of Argyle was watching all
  the time,
But owing to the ground occupied by them he couldn't see
  their line,
Which was unfortunately obstructed by the brow of a hill,
At the thought thereof the Duke's heart with fear did fill.

The hill was occupied by a party of Earl Mar's troops looking
  towards Dunblane,
Which the Earl of Mar no doubt resolved to maintain;
Then the Duke returned to the army, and ordered the drums
  to beat,
But an hour elapsed before his army were ready Mar's to meet.

As soon as the Earl of Mar perceived Argyle's line was
  partially formed,
He gave orders that Argyle's army should be instantly stormed.
Then Mar placed himself at the head of the clans, and led
  forward his men,
As a noble hero would do, which no one can condemn.

Then he pulled off his hat, which he waved in his right hand,
And when he arrived within pistol-shot the Highlanders
  made a bold stand,
And they poured in a volley upon the English infantry,
And to the dismay of the Highlanders the English returned
  fire instantly.

And to the horror of the Highlanders Alan Muidartach was
 wounded mortally,
Then he was carried off the field, a most pitiful sight to see;
And as his men clustered around him they stood aghast,
And before he died he told them to hold their posts fast.

While lamenting the death of the Captain of Clanranald
 most pitifully,
Glengarry at this juncture sprang forward right manfully,
And throwing his bonnet into the air, he cried, heroically,
Revenge! revenge! revenge to-day! and mourning to-morrow
 ye shall see!

No sooner had he pronounced these words than the High
 landers rushed forward, sword in hand,
Upon the royal battalions with the utmost fury, which they
 could not withstand,
And with their broadswords among the enemy they spread
 death and dismay,
Until the three battalions on Argyle's left wing instantly
 gave way.

Then a complete rout ensued, and the Earl of Mar pursued
 them half-a-mile;
Then he ordered his men to halt and rest a while,
Until he should put them into order right speedily,
Then follow the enemy at the double-march and complete
 the victory.

Then the Highlanders chased them and poured in a volley,
Besides they hewed them down with their broadswords
 mercilessly;
But somehow both armies got mixed together, and a general
 rout ensued,
While the Highlanders eagerly the English army hotly pursued.

The success on either side is doubtful to this day,
And all that can be said is, both armies ran away;
And on whichsoever side success lay it was toward the
   Government,
And to allay all doubts about which party won, we mu
   feel content.

EXECUTION OF JAMES GRAHAM, MARQUIS OF MONTROSE

'Twas in the year of 1650, and on the twenty-first of May,
The city of Edinburgh was put into a state of dismay
By the noise of drums and trumpets, which on the air arose,
That the great sound attracted the notice of Montrose.

Who enquired at the Captain of the guard the cause of it,
Then the officer told him, as he thought most fit,
That the Parliament dreading an attempt might be made to
   rescue him,
The soldiers were called out to arms, and that had made the din.

Do I, said Montrose, continue such a terror still?
Now when these good men are about my blood to spill,
But let them look to themselves, for after I am dead,
Their wicked consciences will be in continual dread.

After partaking of a hearty breakfast, he commenced his
   toilet,
Which, in his greatest trouble, he seldom did forget.
And while in the act of combing his hair,
He was visited by the Clerk Register, who made him stare,

When he told him he shouldn't be so particular with his
   head,
For in a few hours he would be dead;
But Montrose replied, While my head is my own I'll dress
   it at my ease,
And to-morrow, when it becomes yours, treat it as you please.

He was waited upon by the Magistrates of the city,
But, alas! for him they had no pity.
He was habited in a superb cloak, ornamented with gold and
   silver lace;
And before the hour of execution an immense assemblage of
   people were round the place.

From the prison, bareheaded, in a cart, they conveyed him
   along the Watergate
To the place of execution on the High Street, where about
   thirty thousand people did wait,
Some crying and sighing, a most pitiful sight to see,
All waiting patiently to see the executioner hang Montrose,
   a man of high degree.

Around the place of execution, all of them were deeply
   affected,
But Montrose, the noble hero, seemed not the least dejected;
And when on the scaffold he had, says his biographer
   Wishart,
Such a grand air and majesty, which made the people start.

As the fatal hour was approaching when he had to bid the
   world adieu,
He told the executioner to make haste and get quickly
   through,
But the executioner smiled grimly, but spoke not a word,
Then he tied the Book of Montrose's Wars round his neck
   with a cord.

Then he told the executioner his foes would remember him hereafter,
And he was as well pleased as if his Majesty had made him Knight of the Garter;
Then he asked to be allowed to cover his head,
But he was denied permission, yet he felt no dread.

He then asked leave to keep on his cloak,
But was also denied, which was a most grievous stroke;
Then he told the Magistrates, if they could invent any more tortures for him,
He would endure them all for the cause he suffered, and think it no sin.

On arriving at the top of the ladder with great firmness,
His heroic appearance greatly did the bystanders impress,
Then Montrose asked the executioner how long his body would be suspended,
Three hours was the answer, but Montrose was not the least offended.

Then he presented the executioner with three or four pieces of gold,
Whom he freely forgave, to his honour be it told,
And told him to throw him off as soon as he uplifted his hands,
While the executioner watched the fatal signal, and in amazement stands.

And on the noble patriot raising his hands, the executioner began to cry,
Then quickly he pulled the rope down from the gibbet on high,
And around Montrose's neck he fixed the rope very gently,
And in an instant the great Montrose was launched into eternity.

Then the spectators expressed their disapprobation by a
 general groan,
And they all dispersed quietly, and wended their way home,
And his bitterest enemies that saw his death that day,
Their hearts were filled with sorrow and dismay.

Thus died, at the age of thirty-eight, James Graham,
 Marquis of Montrose,
Who was brought to a premature grave by his bitter foes;
A commander who had acquired great military glory
In a short space of time, which cannot be equalled in story.

BALDOVAN

The scenery of Baldovan
 Is most lovely to see,
Near by Dighty Water,
 Not far from Dundee.

'Tis health for any one
 To be walking there,
O'er the green swards of Baldovan,
 And in the forests fair.

There the blackbird and the mavis
 Together merrily do sing
In the forest of Baldovan,
 Making the woodlands to ring.

'Tis delightful to hear them
 On a fine summer day,
Carolling their cheerful notes
 So blythe and so gay.

Then there's the little loch near by,
 Whereon can be seen every day
Numerous wild ducks swimming
 And quacking in their innocent play.

LOCH LEVEN

Beautiful Loch Leven, near by Kinross,
For a good day's fishing the angler is seldom at a loss,
For the loch it abounds with pike and trout,
Which can be had for the catching without any doubt;
And the scenery around it is most beautiful to be seen,
Especially the Castle, wherein was imprisoned Scotland's
   ill-starred Queen.

Then there's the lofty Lomond Hills on the eastern side,
And the loch is long, very deep, and wide;
Then on the southern side there's Benarty's rugged hills,
And from the tops can be seen the village of Kinross with
   its spinning mills.

The big house of Kinross is very handsome to be seen,
With its beautiful grounds around it, and lime trees so green
And 'tis a magnificent sight to see, on a fine summer
   afternoon,
The bees extracting honey from the leaves when in full
   bloom.

There the tourist can enjoy himself and while away the hours,
Underneath the lime trees shady bowers,
And listen to the humming of the busy bees,
While they are busy gathering honey from the lime trees.

Then there's the old burying ground near by Kinross,
And the dead that lie there turned into dusty dross,
And the gravestones are all in a state of decay,
And the old wall around it is mouldering away.

THE CASTLE OF MAINS

Ancient Castle of the Mains,
With your romantic scenery
And surrounding plains,
Which seem most beautiful to the eye;
And the little rivulet running by,
Which the weary traveller can drink of when he feels dry,
And the heaven's breath smells sweetly there,
And scented perfumes fill the air,
Emanating from the green trees and beautiful wild flowers
   growing there.

There the people can enjoy themselves
And wile away the time,
By admiring the romantic scenery
In the beautiful sunshine;
And pull the little daisy,
As they carelessly recline
Upon the grassy green banks,
Which is most charming to see,
Near by the Castle of the Mains,
Not far from Dundee.

Then there's the old burying-ground,
Most solemn to see,...
And the silent dead reposing silently
Amid the shady trees,
In that beautiful fairy dell
Most lovely to see,
Which in the summer season
Fills the people's hearts with glee,
To hear the birds singing and the humming of the bee.

MONTROSE

Beautiful town of Montrose, I will now commence my
   lay,
And I will write in praise of thee without dismay,
And in spite of all your foes, ...
I will venture to call thee Bonnie Montrose.
Your beautiful Chain Bridge is magnificent to be seen,
Spanning the river Esk, a beautiful tidal stream,
Which abounds with trout and salmon,
Which can be had for the catching without any gammon.

Then as for the Mid Links, it is most beautiful to be
   seen,
And I'm sure is a very nice bowling green,
Where young men can enjoy themselves and inhale the pure
   air,
Emanating from the sea and the beautiful flowers there,
And as for the High Street, it's most beautiful to see,
There's no street can surpass it in the town of Dundee,
Because it is so long and wide, ...
That the people can pass on either side
Without jostling one another or going to any bother.

Beautiful town of Montrose, near by the seaside,
With your fine shops and streets so wide,
'Tis health for the people that in you reside,
Because they do inhale the pure fragrant air,
Emanating from the pure salt wave and shrubberies growing
   there;
And the inhabitants of Montrose ought to feel gay.
Because it is one of the bonniest towns in Scotland at the
   present day.

BROUGHTY FERRY

Ancient Castle of Broughty Ferry
With walls as strong as Londonderry;
Near by the sea-shore,
Where oft is heard and has been heard the cannon's roar
In the present day and days of yore,
Loudly echoing from shore to shore.

From your impregnable ramparts high
Like the loud thunder in the sky,
Enough to frighten a foreign foe away
That would dare to come up the river Tay,
To lay siege to Bonnie Dundee,
I'm sure your cannon-balls would make them flee —

Home again to their own land
Because your cannon shot they could not withstand,
They would soon be glad to get away
From the beautiful shores of the silvery Tay.

Ancient Castle, near by Tayside,
The soldiers ought to feel happy that in you reside,
Because from the top they can have a view of Fife,
Which ought to drown their sorrow and give them fresh life,
And make their spirits feel light and gay
As they view the beautiful scenery of the silvery Tay.

The village of Broughty Ferry is most beautiful to see,
With its stately mansions and productive fishery,
Which is a great boon to the villagers and the people of
　Dundee,
And ought to make them thankful, and unto God to pray
For creating plenty of fish for them in the beautiful Tay.

And the city of Dundee seems beautiful to the eye
With her mill stalks and Old Steeple so high,
Which can be seen on a clear summer day
From the top of Broughty Castle near the mouth of Tay.

Then there's beautiful Reres Hill,
Where the people can ramble at their will
Amongst its beautiful shrubberies and trees so green
Which in the summer season is most charming to be seen,
And ought to drive dull care away,
Because the people can see every clear day
From the top the ships sailing on the silvery Tay.

ROBERT BURNS

Immortal Robert Burns of Ayr,
There's but few poets can with you compare;
Some of your poems and songs are very fine:
To "Mary in Heaven" is most sublime;
And then again in your "Cottar's Saturday Night,"
Your genius there does shine most bright,
As pure as the dewdrops of night.

Your "Tam o' Shanter" is very fine,
Both funny, racy, and divine,
From John o' Groats to Dumfries
All critics consider it to be a masterpiece,
And, also, you have said the same,
Therefore they are not to blame.

And in my own opinion both you and they are right,
For your genius there does sparkle bright,
Which I most solemnly declare
To thee, Immortal Bard of Ayr!

Your "Banks and Braes of Bonnie Doon"
Is sweet and melodious in its tune,
And the poetry is moral and sublime,
And in my opinion nothing can be more fine.

Your "Scots wha hae wi' Wallace bled"
Is most beautiful to hear sung or read;
For your genius there does shine as bright,
Like unto the stars of night . . . . .

Immortal Bard of Ayr! I must conclude, my muse
To speak in praise of thee does not refuse,
For you were a mighty poet, few could with you compare,
And also an honour to Scotland, for your genius it is rare.

ADVENTURES OF ROBERT THE BRUCE

King Robert the Bruce's deadly enemy, John of Lorn,
Joined the English with eight hundred Highlanders one fine morn,
All strong, hardy, and active fearless mountaineers,
But Bruce's men attacked them with swords and spears.

And while they were engaged, a new enemy burst upon them,
Like a torrent of raging water rushing down a rocky glen:
It was John of Lorn and his Highlanders that came upon them,
So the tide of battle was too much for them to stem.

And with savage yells they made the valley ring,
Then made a long circuit, and stole in behind the King,
Whirling their broadswords and Lochaber axes left and right;
And the enemy being thrice their number, they relinquished the fight.

Then to a certain house Bruce quickly hied,
And sitting by the door the housewife he spied;
And she asked him who he was, and he said, A wanderer,
Then she said, All wanderers are welcome here, kind sir.

Then the King said, Good dame, tell me the reason why,
How you respect all wanderers that chance to pass by,
And for whose sake you bear such favour to homeless men!
Then she said, King Robert the bruce, if you want to ken,

The lawful King of this country, whom I hope to see;
Then Bruce said, My good woman, your King stands before
  thee
And she said, Ah! sire, where are your men gone?
Then the King told her that he's come alone.

Then she said, Ah, my lawful King, this must not be,
For I have two stout sons, and they shall follow thee,
And fight to the death for your Majesty,
Aye, in faith, my good King, by land or sea.

Then she brought her sons before the King, and thus did say,
Now swear, my sons, to be true to your King without dismay;
Then they knelt and cried, Mother, we'll do as you desire,
We willingly will fight on behalf of our noble sire.

Who has been hunted like a felon by night and by day,
By foul plotters devising to take his life away;
But God will protect him in the midst of the strife,
And, mother dear, we'll fight for him during life.

Then the King said, Noble lads, it's you shall follow me,
And ye shall be near me by land or sea,
And for your loyalty towards me your mother I'll reward;
When all on a sudden the tramping of horses was heard.

Then the King heard voices he knew full well,
But what had fetched his friends there he couldn't tell;
'Twas Edward his brother and Lord Douglas, with one
    hundred and fifty men,
That had travelled far, to find their King, o'er mountain
    and glen.

And when they met they conversed on the events of the day,
Then the King unto them quickly did say,
If we knew where the enemy were, we would work them skaith;
Then Lord James said, I'll lead you where they are, by my faith.

Then they marched upon the enemy just as the morning broke,
To a farm house where they were lodged, and, with one bold
    stroke,
They, the Scots, rushed in and killed two-thirds of them dead;
And such was the life, alas! King Robert the Bruce led!

A TALE OF THE SEA

A pathetic tale of the sea I will unfold,
Enough to make one's blood run cold;
Concerning four fishermen cast adrift in a dory.
As I've been told, I'll relate the story.

'Twas on the 8th April, on the afternoon of that day,
That the little village of Louisburg was thrown into a wild
    state of dismay,
And the villagers flew to the beach in a state of wild uproar
And in a dory they found four men were cast ashore.

Then the villagers, in surprise, assembled about the dory,
And they found that the bottom of the boat was gory;
Then their hearts were seized with sudden dread,
When they discovered that two of the men were dead.

And the two survivors were exhausted from exposure,
   hunger, and cold,
Which caused the spectators to shudder when them they did
   behold;
And with hunger the poor men couldn't stand on their feet,
They felt so weakly on their legs for want of meat.

They were carried to a boarding-house without delay,
But those that were looking on were stricken with dismay,
When the remains of James and Angus M'Donald were found
   in the boat,
Likewise three pieces of flesh in a pool of blood afloat.

Angus M'Donald's right arm was missing from the elbow,
And the throat was cut in a sickening manner, which filled
   the villagers hearts with woe,
Especially when they saw two pieces of flesh had been cut
   from each thigh,
'Twas then the kind-hearted villagers did murmur and sigh.

Angus M'Donald must have felt the pangs of hunger before
   he did try
To cut two pieces of flesh from James M'Donald's thigh;
But, Oh, heaven! the pangs of hunger are very hard to thole,
And anything that's eatable is precious unto an hungry soul.

Alas! it is most pitiful and horrible to think,
That with hunger Christians will each other's blood drink,
And eat each other's flesh to save themselves from starvation;
But the pangs of hunger makes them mad, and drives them
   to desperation.

An old American soldier, that had passed through the Civil War,
Declared the scene surpassed anything he's seen by far,
And at the sight, the crowd in horror turned away,
Which no doubt they will remember for many a day.

Colin Chisholm, one of the survivors, was looking very pale,
Stretched on a sofa, at the boarding-house, making his wail;
Poor fellow! his feet were greatly swollen, and with a melancholy air,
He gave the following account of the distressing affair:

We belonged to the American fishing schooner, named "Cicely,"
And our captain was a brave man, called M'Kenzie;
And the vessel had fourteen hands altogether,
And during the passage we had favourable weather.

'Twas on March the 17th we sailed from Gloucester, on the Wednesday,
And all our hearts felt buoyant and gay;
And we arrived on the Western banks on the succeeding Tuesday,
While the time unto us seemed to pass merrily away.

About eight o'clock in the morning, we left the vessel in a dory,
And I hope all kind Christians will take heed to my story:
Well, while we were at our work, the sky began to frown,
And with a dense fog we were suddenly shut down.

Then we hunted and shouted, and every nerve did strain,
Thinking to find our schooner, but, alas! it was all in vain:
Because the thick fog hid the vessel from our view,
And to keep ourselves warm we closely to each other drew.

We had not one drop of water, nor provisions of any kind,
Which, alas! soon began to tell on our mind;
Especially upon James M'Donald, who was very thinly clad,
And with the cold and hunger he felt almost mad.

And looking from the stern where he was lying,
He said, Good-bye, mates, Oh! I am dying!
Poor fellow, we kept his body, thinking the rest of us would
  be saved,
Then, with hunger, Angus M'Donald began to cry and
  madly raved.

And he cried, Oh, God! send us some kind of meat,
Because I'm resolved to have something to eat;
Oh! do not let us starve on the briny flood,
Or else I will drink of poor Jim's blood.

Then he suddenly seized his knife and cut off poor Jim's arm,
Not thinking in his madness he'd done any harm;
Then poor Jim's blood he did drink, and his flesh did eat,
Declaring that the blood tasted like cream, and was a treat.

Then he asked me to taste it, saying, It was good without
  doubt,
Then I tasted it, but in disgust I instantly spat it out;
Saying, If I was to die within an hour on the briny flood,
I would neither eat the flesh nor drink the blood.

Then in the afternoon again he turned to me,
Saying, I'm going to cut Jim's throat for more blood d'ye see;
Then I begged of him, for God's sake, not to cut the throat of
  poor Jim,
But he cried, Ha! ha! to save my own life I consider it no sin.

I tried to prevent him, but he struck me without dismay,
And cut poor Jim's throat in defiance of me, or all I could say,
Also a piece of flesh from each thigh, and began to eat away,
But poor fellow he sickened about noon, and died on the
  Sunday.

Now it is all over, and I will thank God all my life,
Who has preserved me and my mate, M'Eachern, in the
  midst of danger and strife
And I hope that all landsmen of low and high degree,
Will think of the hardships of poor mariners while at sea.

JOTTINGS OF LONDON

As I stood upon London Bridge and viewed the mighty throng
Of thousands of people in cabs and 'busses rapidly whirling
  along,
All furiously driving to and fro,
Up one street and down another as quick as they could go:

Then I was struck with the discordant sounds of human
  voices there,
Which seemed to me like wild geese cackling in the air:
And the river Thames is a most beautiful sight,
To see the steamers sailing upon it by day and by night.

And the Tower of London is most gloomy to behold,
And the crown of England lies there, begemmed with
  precious stones and gold;
King Henry the Sixth was murdered there by the Duke of
  Glo'ster,
And when he killed him with his sword he called him an
  imposter.

St Paul's Cathedral is the finest building that ever I did see,
There's no building can surpass it in the city of Dundee,
Because it's magnificent to behold,
With its beautiful dome and spire glittering like gold.

And as for Nelson's Monument that stands in Trafalgar
  Square,
It is a most stately monument I most solemnly declare,
And towering defiantly very high,
Which arrests strangers' attention while passing by.

Then there's two beautiful water-fountains spouting up very
  high,
Where the weary traveller can drink when he feels dry;
And at the foot of the monument there's three bronze lions
  in grand array,
Enough to make the stranger's heart throb with dismay.

Then there's Mr Spurgeon, a great preacher, which no one
  dare gainsay,
I went to hear him preach on the Sabbath-day,
And he made my heart feel light and gay,
When I heard him preach and pray.

And the Tabernacle was crowded from ceiling to floor,
And many were standing outside the door;
He is an eloquent preacher I honestly declare,
And I was struck with admiration as on him I did stare.

Then there's Petticoat Lane I venture to say,
It's a wonderful place on the Sabbath-day;
There wearing-apparel can be bought to suit the young or old,
For the ready cash, silver, coppers, or gold.

Oh! mighty city of London! you are wonderful to see,
And thy beauties no doubt fill the tourist's heart with glee;
But during my short stay, and while wandering there,
Mr Spurgeon was the only man I heard speaking proper
  English I do declare.

ANNIE MARSHALL THE FOUNDING

Annie Marshall was a foundling, and lived in Downderry,
And was trained up by a coast-guardsman, kind-hearted and merry,
And he loved Annie Marshall as dear as his life,
And he resolved to make her his own loving wife.

The night was tempestuous, most terrific, and pitch dark,
When Matthew Pengelly rescued Annie Marshall from an ill-fated barque,
But her parents were engulfed in the briny deep,
Which caused poor Annie at times to sigh and weep.

One day Matthew asked Annie if she would be his wife,
And Annie replied, I never thought of it in all my life;
Yes, my wife, Annie, replied Matthew, hold hard a bit,
Remember, Annie, I've watched you grow up, and consider you most fit.

Poor Annie did not speak, she remained quite mute,
And with agitation she trembled from head to foot,
The poor girl was in a dilemma, she knew not what to say,
And owing to Matthew training her, she couldn't say him nay.

Oh! Matthew, I'm afraid I would not make you a good wife,
And in that respect there would be too much strife,
And the thought thereof, believe me, makes me feel ill,
Because I'm unfit to be thy wife, Matthew, faltered the poor girl.

Time will prove that, dear Annie, but why are you so calm?
Then Annie put her hand shyly into Matthew's brown palm.
Just then the flashing lightning played upon Annie's face.
And the loud thunder drowned Matthew's words as Annie left the place.

But Matthew looked after her as she went home straightway,
And his old heart felt light and gay,
As he looked forward for his coming marriage day,
Because he knew that Annie Marshall couldn't say him nay.

Then the sky grew dark, and the sea lashed itself into foam,
But he heeded it not as he sat there alone,
Till the sound of a gun came booming o'er the sea,
Then Matthew had to attend to his duty immediately.

A ship, he muttered, Lord, help them! and coming right in by the sound,
And in a few minutes she will run aground.
And the vessel was dashed against the rocks with her helpless crew,
Then in hot haste for assistance Matthew instantly flew.

Then Matthew returned with a few men all willing to lend their aid,
But amongst them all Matthew seemed the least afraid;
Then an old man cried, Save my boy, for his mother's sake,
Oh! Matthew, try and save him, or my heart will break!

I will, Heaven helping me, Matthew said solemnly,
Come, bear a hand, mates, and lower me over the cliff quietly;
Then Matthew was lowered with ropes into what seemed a watery grave,
At the risk of his own life, old Jonathan Bately's on to ave.

So Matthew Pengelly saved Jonathan Bately's son,
And the old man thanked God and Matthew for what he had done,
And the mother's heart was full of gratitude and joy,
For the restoration of her darling boy.

So Matthew resolved to marry Annie Marshall,
But first he d go to sea whatever did befall,
To earn a few pounds to make the marriage more grand,
So he joined a whaling vessel and went to Greenland.

And while Matthew was away at Greenland,
David Bately wanted to marry Annie Marshall right offhand,
But Annie refused to marry David Bately,
So in anger David Bately went another voyage to sea.

A few nights after David Bately had gone to sea,
Annie's thoughts reverted to Matthew Pengelly,
And as she sat in the Downderry station watching the
   boiling waves below,
The wind blew a terrific gale, which filled her heart with woe.

And as she sat there the big waves did loudly roar,
When a man cried, Help! help! there's a corpse washed ashore;
Then Annie rushed madly to the little beach,
And when she saw the corpse she gave a loud screech.

So there is but little more to tell of this sad history,
Only that Annie Marshall mourned long for Matthew
   Pengelly,
Who had floated home to be buried amongst his own kin,
But, alas! the rest of the crew were buried in the sea, save
   him.

BILL BOWLS THE SAILOR

'Twas about the beginning of the present century,
Bill Bowls was pressed, and sent to sea;
And conveyed on board the Waterwitch without delay,
Scarce getting time to bid farewell to the villagers of Fairway.

And once on board the "Waterwitch," he resolved to do his
 duty,
And God willing, he'd marry Nelly Blyth, the village beauty;
And he'd fight for Old England, like a jolly British tar,
And he'd think of Nelly Blyth during the war.

The poor fellow little imagined what he had to go through,
But in all his trials at sea, he never did rue;
No; the brave tar became reconciled to his fate,
And he felt proud of his commander, Captain Ward the great.

And on board the "Waterwitch" was Tom Riggles, his old
 comrade,
And with such a one as Tom Riggles he seldom felt afraid,
Because the stories they told on board made the time fly away,
And made the hearts of their messmates feel light and gay.

'Twas on a sunny morning, and clear to the view,
Captain Ward the close attention of his men he drew:
Look! he cried, there's two Frenchmen of war on our right,
Therefore, prepare my men immediately to commence the
 fight.

Then the "Waterwitch" was steered to the ship most near,
While every man resolved to sell his life most dear;
But the French commander, disinclined to commence the fight,
Ordered his men to put on a press of canvas and take to flight.

But Captain Ward quickly gave the order to fire,
Then Bill Bowls cried, Now we'll get fighting to our heart's
 desire!
And for an hour and more a running fight was maintained,
Until the two ships of the enemy near upon the "Waterwitch"
 gained.

Captain Ward walked the deck with a firm tread,
When a shot from the enemy pierced the ship's side above
   his head;
And with a splinter Bill Bowls was wounded on the left arm,
And he cried, Death to the frog-eaters! they have done me
   little harm.

Then Captain Ward cried, Fear not, we will win the day,
Now, courage my men, pour in broadsides without delay;
Then they sailed round the "St Denis" and the "Gloire,"
And in at their cabin windows they poured a deadly fire.

The effect on the two ships was fearful to behold,
But still the Frenchmen stuck to their guns with courage, be
   it told;
And the crash and din of artillery was deafening to the ear,
And the cries of the wounded men on deck were pitiful to hear.

Then Captain Ward to his men did say,
We must board these French ships without dismay;
Then he seized his cutlass, as he fearlessly spoke,
And jumped on board the "St Denis" in the midst of the
   smoke.

Then Bill Bowls and Tom Riggles quickly followed him,
Then hand to hand the battle in earnest did begin;
And the men sprang upon their foes and beat them back,
And they hauled down their colours, and hoisted the Union Jack.

But the men on board the "St Denis" fought desperately hard,
But, alas! as the "St Denis" was captured, a ball struck
   Captain Ward
Right on the forehead, and he fell dead with a groan
And for the death of Captain Ward the sailors did cry and moan.

Then the first lieutenant, who was standing near by,
Loudly to the men did cry:
Come men, and carry your noble commander to his cabin
  below,
But there is one consolation, we have beaten the foe.

And thus fell Captain Ward in the prime of his life,
And I hope he is now in the better land, free from strife:
But, alas! 'tis sad to think he was buried in the mighty deep,
Where too many of our brave seamen do silently sleep.

The "St Denis" and the "Gloire" were towed to Gibraltar,
  the nearest port,
But by the capturing of them, they felt but little sport,
Because, for the loss of Captain Ward, the men felt woe-begone,
Because in bravery, they said, he was next to Admiral Nelson.

YOUNG MUNRO THE SAILOR

'Twas on a sunny morning in the month of May,
I met a pretty damsel on the banks o' the Tay;
I said, My charming fair one, come tell to me I pray,
Why you do walk alone on the banks o' the Tay.

She said, Kind sir, pity me, for I am in great woe
About my young sailor lad, whose name is James Munro;
It's he has been long at sea, seven years from this day,
And I come here sometimes to weep for him that's far, far
  away

Lovely creature, cease your weeping and consent to marry
   me,
And my houses and all my land I will give to thee,
And we shall get married without any delay,
And live happy and contented on the banks o' the Tay.

Believe me, my sweet lady, I pity the sailor's wife,
For I think she must lead a very unhappy life;
Especially on a stormy night, I'm sure she cannot sleep,
Thinking about her husband whilst on the briny deep.

Oh, sir! it is true, what you to me have said,
But I must be content with the choice I've made;
For Munro he's young and handsome, I will ne'er deny,
And if I don't get him for a husband, believe me, I will
   die.

Because, when last we parted, we swore to be true,
And I will keep my troth, which lovers ought to do;
And I will pray for his safe return by night and by day,
That God may send him safe home to the banks o' the
   Tay.

Forgive me, noble heart, for asking to marry you,
I was only trying your love, if it was really true;
But I've found your love is pure towards your sailor lad,
And the thought thereof, believe me, makes my heart feel
   glad.

As homeward we retraced our steps her heart seemed
   glad,
In hopes of seeing again her brave sailor lad,
Who had promised to marry her when he would return,
So I bade her keep up her spirits and no longer mourn.

Dear creature, the lass that's true to her sweetheart deserves
  great praise,
and I hope young Munro and you will spend many happy
  days,
For unto him I know you will ever prove true,
And perchance when he comes home he will marry you.

What you have said, kind sir, I hope will come true,
And if it does, I'll make it known to you;
And you must come to the marriage, which you musn't
  gainsay,
And dance and rejoice with us on the marriage-day.

When we arrived in Dundee she bade me good-bye,
Then I told her where I lived, while she said with a sigh,
Kind sir, I will long remember that morning in May,
When I met you by chance on the banks o' the Tay.

When three months were past her sailor lad came home,
And she called to see me herself alone,
And she invited me to her marriage without delay,
Which was celebrated with great pomp the next day.

So I went to the marriage with my heart full of joy,
And I wished her prosperity with her sailor boy;
And I danced and sang till daylight, and then came away,
Leaving them happy and contented on the banks o' the Tay.

So all ye pretty fair maids, of high or low degree,
Be faithful to your sweethearts when they have gone to sea,
And never be in doubts of them when they are far away,
Because they might return and marry you some unexpected
  day.

TRIBUTE TO MR MURPHY AND THE BLUE RIBBON ARMY

All hail to Mr Murphy, he is a hero brave,
That has crossed the mighty Atlantic wave,
For what purpose let me pause and think—
I answer, to warn the people not to taste strong drink.

And, I'm sure, if they take his advice, they never will rue
The day they joined the Blue Ribbon Army in the year 1882;
And I hope to their colours they will always prove true,
And shout, Hurrah! for Mr Murphy and the Ribbon of Blue.

What is strong drink? Let me think — I answer 'tis a thing
From whence the majority of evils spring,
And causes many a fireside with boisterous talk to ring,
And leaves behind it a deadly sting.

Some people do say it is good when taken in moderation,
But, when taken to excess, it leads to tribulation,
Also to starvation and loss of reputation,
Likewise your eternal soul's damnation.

The drunkard, he says he can't give it up,
For I must confess temptation's in the cup;
But he wishes to God it was banished from the land,
While he holds the cup in his trembling hand.

And he exclaims in the agony of his soul—
Oh, God, I cannot myself control
From this most accurs'd cup!
Oh, help me, God, to give it up!

Strong drink to the body can do no good;
It defiles the blood, likewise the food,
And causes the drunkard with pain to groan,
Because it extracts the marrow from the bone:

And hastens him on to a premature grave,
Because to the cup he is bound a slave;
For the temptation is hard to thole,
And by it he will lose his immortal soul.

The more's the pity, I must say,
That so many men and women are by it led astray,
And decoyed from the paths of virtue and led on to vice
By drinking too much alcohol and acting unwise.

Good people all, of every degree,
I pray, ye all be warned by me:
I advise ye all to pause and think,
And never more to taste strong drink.

Because the drunkard shall never inherit the kingdom of God
And whosoever God loves he chastens with his rod:
Therefore, be warned, and think in time,
And don't drink any more whisky, rum, or wine.

But go at once — make no delay,
And join the Blue Ribbon Army without dismay,
And rally round Mr Murphy, and make a bold stand,
And help to drive the Bane of Society from our land.

I wish Mr Murphy every success,
Hoping he will make rapid progress; And to the Blue Ribbon Army may he always prove true,
And adhere to his colours — the beautiful blue.